8/1

How Are They Made?
Bottles and Jars

Wendy Blaxland

Marshall Cavendish
Benchmark

New York

Website: www.marshallcavendish.us

This publication represents the opinions and views of the author based on Wendy Blaxland's personal experience, knowledge, and research. The information in this book serves as a general guide only. The author and publisher have used their best efforts in preparing this book and disclaim liability rising directly and indirectly from the use and application of this book.

Other Marshall Cavendish Offices:
Marshall Cavendish Ltd. 5th Floor, 32-38 Saffron Hill, London EC1N 8 FH, UK • Marshall Cavendish International (Asia) Private Limited, 1 New Industrial Road, Singapore 536196 • Marshall Cavendish International (Thailand) Co Ltd. 253 Asoke, 12th Flr, Sukhumvit 21 Road, Klongtoey Nua, Wattana, Bangkok 10110, Thailand • Marshall Cavendish (Malaysia) Sdn Bhd, Times Subang, Lot 46, Subang Hi-Tech Industrial Park, Batu Tiga, 40000 Shah Alam, Selangor Darul Ehsan, Malaysia

Marshall Cavendish is a trademark of Times Publishing Limited

All websites were available and accurate when this book was sent to press.

Library of Congress Cataloging-in-Publication Data

Blaxland, Wendy.
    Bottles and jars / Wendy Blaxland.
      p. cm. — (How are they made?)
    Includes index.
    Summary: "Discusses how bottles and jars are made"—Provided by publisher.
    ISBN 978-0-7614-4752-8
    1. Bottles—Juvenile literature. 2. Plastic bottles—Juvenile literature. 3. Glass blowing and working—Juvenile literature. I. Title.
    TP866.B585 2011
666'.192--dc22

                                                                          2009040080

First published in 2010 by
MACMILLAN EDUCATION AUSTRALIA PTY LTD
15–19 Claremont Street, South Yarra 3141

Visit our website at www.macmillan.com.au or go directly to www.macmillanlibrary.com.au

Associated companies and representatives throughout the world.

Copyright © Wendy Blaxland 2010

Edited by Anna Fern
Text and cover design by Cristina Neri, Canary Graphic Design
Page layout by Peggy Bampton, Relish Graphic
Photo research by Jes Senbergs
Map by Damien Demaj, DEMAP; modified by Cristina Neri, Canary Graphic Design

Printed in the United States

Acknowledgments
The author would like to thank the following for their expert advice: Peter Bury, Plastics and Chemicals Industries Association, Abbotsford, Victoria, Australia; Glass Packaging Institute, Alexandria, Virginia, United States; Adam Niederer, Amcor Australasia Glass Division; Greg Robinson, Ball Corporation, Broomfield, Colorado, United States; Thomas Rae Southall, The Society of the Plastics Industry, Washington, United States; UN Statistics Division – Economics Statistics Branch, New York, United States.

The author and the publisher are grateful to the following for permission to reproduce copyright material:

Front cover photographs: Bottle of olive oil, © Ben Neumann/istockphoto (left); jar of lollies, Flyfloor/istockphoto (top); plastic bottle of water, © Luis Fernandez/istockphoto (right); pink jar, © Zoran Kolundzija/istockphoto (middle); perfume bottle, © Sergey Lemeshencko/istockphoto (bottom right).

Photographs courtesy of:
© Werner Forman/Corbis, **7**; © Robert Garvey/Corbis, **9**; © Bob Krist/Corbis, **17**; © Owaki/Kulla/Corbis, **20**; © Ed Wheeler/ Corbis, **10**; Rob Cruse, **14**, **30**; Olivier Morin/AFP/Getty Images, **6**; D. S. Axley/iStockphoto, **5** (top left); J. S. Cook/iStockphoto, **25** (top); Flyfloor/iStockphoto, **13**; Suzi Foo/iStockphoto, **5** (bottom); Luis Fernandez/iStockphoto, **3** (bottom), **12**; Zoran Kolundzija/ iStockphoto, **25**; Simon Kr/iStockphoto, **5** (top right); Sergey Lemeshencko/iStockphoto, **3** (top); Ben Neumann/iStockphoto, **4** (top), **15**; Prill/iStockphoto, **8**; © Simon Belcher/Alamy/Photolibrary, **24**; © Joe Hula/Alamy/Photolibrary, **22**; © JG Photography/ Alamy/Photolibrary, **4** (bottom); © H. Mark Weidman Photography/Alamy/Photolibrary, **18**; James L. Amos/Photolibrary.com, **27**; Polly Eltes/Photolibrary.com, **11**; PPS/Photolibrary.com, **21**; Ton Kinsbergen/Science Photo Library/Photolibrary, **16**, **23**; Philippe Psaila/Science Photo Library/Photolibrary, **28**; Y. Beaulieu Publiphoto Diffusion/Science Photo Library/Photolibrary, **29**; Geoff Tompkinson/Science Photo Library/Photolibrary, **19**; Reuters/Picture Media/Nicky Loh, **26**.

While every care has been taken to trace and acknowledge copyright, the publisher tenders their apologies for any accidental infringement where copyright has proved untraceable. Where the attempt has been unsuccessful, the publisher welcomes information that would redress the situation.

135642

Contents

Glossary Words

When a word is printed in **bold**, you can look up its meaning in the Glossary on page 31.

From Raw Materials to Products

Everything we use is made from raw materials from Earth. These are called natural resources. People take natural resources and make them into useful products.

Bottles and Jars

Bottles and jars are containers for holding liquids and other materials, such as powders, which can be poured through an opening. Jars are generally shaped like cylinders and have wide openings, or mouths. Bottles come in a variety of shapes, with much smaller openings. The mouths of bottles and jars are plugged with glass or other stoppers, **corked**, or capped with metal or plastic caps.

The main raw materials for making most bottles and jars are glass and plastic. These substances are made in factories from minerals dug from Earth. Bottles and jars may also be made of other materials such as clay, metal, or even wood.

The drinks shelves in a supermarket contain many types of bottles made from different materials.

Bottles and jars are used as packaging for food, drinks, and other items.

Guess What!

Jar comes originally from the Arabic word *jarrah*, an earthenware water container. *Bottle* came from the Old French word *botelle*, which developed from the Latin word *butticula*, meaning "little cask." Some liquids used to be stored in wooden casks.

Why Do We Need Bottles and Jars?

Bottles and jars are containers that protect their contents from spilling or spoiling. They keep what is inside them clean, safe, and fit to be sold.

Most bottles and jars are used in the food and drink industries. They also hold **cosmetics**, health-care products, and other substances, such as oil. They range in size from huge demijohns and giant cookie barrels to tiny medicine bottles.

Glass bottles and jars have been largely replaced in the food industry by plastic bottles, metal cans, and cardboard cartons. However, wine, beer, and sometimes mineral water continue to be sold in glass bottles. Glass jars are still used for **preserving** food, especially at home, as well as for luxury or special items.

The History of Bottles and Jars

Glass bottles developed over thousands of years. At first they were hard to make and expensive, so they were sold empty and buyers washed and reused them. Bottles became cheaper when new ways of **manufacturing** developed in the 1800s. They began to be sold filled with different products. Plastic bottles have been used widely only since 1947.

Question & Answer

Why did Queen Elizabeth I appoint an Official Uncorker of Ocean Bottles?

In the 1500s people sent messages in bottles. Because the bottles that washed up on English shores might contain official secrets, Elizabeth named an Official Uncorker. Anyone else who opened a bottle would be hanged!

Bottles and Jars Through the Ages

5000 BCE
Traders from Phoenicia (now coastal Middle East) develop glass bottles for perfume.

1500 BCE
Egyptians sculpt glass into bottles for cosmetics, ointments, and perfumes.

200 BCE
Bottles are made in China, Egypt, and the Middle East by pouring molten glass into **molds**.

1000 BCE
Glass pouring techniques are invented.

300 BCE
Syrians discover that **molten** glass can be made into a bottle by blowing air into it through a blowpipe.

5000 BCE 1500 BCE 1000 BCE 300 BCE 200 BCE

The invention of glass blowing meant making glass bottles became easier and cheaper.

6

Glass bottles from ancient Egyptian times were used to hold cosmetics.

1862
Englishman Alexander Parkes shows the first man-made plastic, Parkesine, at the London Great International Exhibition.

1960s Plastic bottles become popular because of cheaper HDPE plastic.

1842
John Kilner's glass factory in Yorkshire, England, makes jars for bottling preserves.

1652 CE
Englishman Sir Kenelm Digby makes the first wine bottle in a wooden mold.

1 CE

1600

1800

1900

2000

27 BCE–476 CE
Romans spread glassmaking skills throughout their empire.

1903
In the United States, Michael J. Owens invents an automatic bottle-forming machine. Glass bottles can now be made more quickly and cheaply.

1947
Blow-molding machines are invented. Plastic bottles are first sold to the public.

1970s
Glass bottles are widely recycled.

1980s
Plastic bottles are widely recycled.

What Are Bottles and Jars Made From?

Bottles and jars are generally made either of glass or different sorts of plastic, depending on what they are used for. Plastic bottles and jars are mostly sealed with plastic caps. Glass bottles may be sealed with corks or aluminum or plastic caps. Stoppers can also be made of other materials such as wood, pottery, and metal.

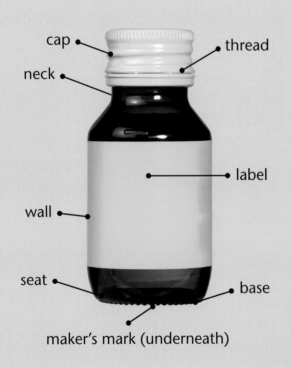

cap

thread

neck

label

wall

seat

base

maker's mark (underneath)

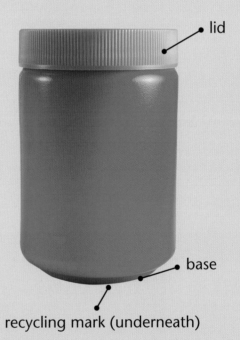

lid

base

recycling mark (underneath)

Materials

Making glass for containers needs certain materials in the right quantities. Plastics for containers are made from oil or gas, with different chemicals added. As with the making of all products, energy is used to run the machines that help mine the oil and minerals, manufacture glass and plastic, and make and decorate the bottles and jars.

Sand, the main ingredient in glass, is mined from the ground.

Materials Used to Make Bottles and Jars

Materials for Glass	Purpose and Qualities
Sand (silica dioxide)	The main ingredient of glass. It is melted to make glass.
Recycled glass or **cullet**	Brings down the melting temperature of new glass.
Soda ash or potash	Lowers the melting point of glass.
Limestone	Helps strengthen glass.
Metal compounds	Add color to glass.
Cork, aluminum, plastics	Used for bottle stoppers and caps.
PETE (polyethylene terephthalate)	Used for drink bottles.
HDPE (high density polyethylene)	Most widely used material for plastic bottles. **Flexible** and cheap.
LDPE (low density polyethylene)	Used mainly for squeeze bottles. Less **rigid** than HDPE.
PVC (polyvinyl chloride)	Used to hold cosmetics, shampoo, oil, and vinegar. Can be dissolved by some chemicals.
Polypropylene	Used for jars filled with heated products. Can stand high temperatures.
Polystyrene	Used for dry foods. Rigid, but may break when hit.

Bottle and Jar Design

Bottles and jars are usually sold containing products, so designers choose the container's material and size to match what it holds. Designers can make a product stand out by choosing different shapes, colors, or decorations for the container.

Another important design influence is cost. Designers constantly try to design containers that use less material and cost less to make. Many designers do their work more quickly, and therefore much more cheaply, using computer-aided design. Computer programs can show the shape, color, size, and character of a product design without the need to make expensive samples.

Ideally, containers should be lightweight, cheap to produce, and attractive.

Guess What!

In the 1800s, when chemical poisons became available, many people died from accidentally drinking them. So, to warn people, manufacturers designed special poison bottles. They were often bright blue or with bumps you could feel in the dark.

Antique glass bottles are sometimes decorated with etched or cut patterns.

Glass or Plastic?

Glass containers are heavy, bulky, and shatter easily. Light, cheap plastics have therefore replaced glass for most bottles and jars since the 1960s. Plastic containers are mostly seen as disposable. There are also concerns that some plastic containers may harm or cause a chemical change in their contents. Glass, however, lasts for thousands of years, and glass containers will not damage their contents. Bottles for wine and beer and luxuries such as perfume are still generally made of glass.

Bottle and Jar Decoration

Older decorative techniques for glass containers include **embossing** to make a surface pattern stand out, and **etching** the glass with acid to make frosted patterns. Newer techniques used to decorate and label both glass and plastic include transfers, screen-printing, and even coatings that change color with different temperatures or light levels. Glass bottles often have plastic sleeves glued or shrunk onto them with heat.

From Glass and Plastic to Bottles and Jars

The process of making everyday objects such as bottles and jars from raw materials involves a number of steps. In the first stage, the oil and minerals are mined and glass and plastic made. The second stage involves shaping the bottles and jars in molds. In the final stage, the bottles and jars are checked, cleaned, filled, sealed, and labeled.

Stage 1: Making Glass and Plastic

Plastic

Oil and natural gas are mined.

↓

Next, the oil and gas are broken down and made into **polymers**.

↓

Lastly, the raw plastic is made into small beads, called **nurdles**.

Glass

Sand and limestone are mined. Soda ash is mined or made.

↓

These materials are then melted in a very hot **furnace**.

↓

Next, the molten glass is cut into gobs or chunks.

Stage 2: Forming Bottles and Jars

Plastic

First, the plastic nurdles are melted.

↓

Then they are made into shapes called **preforms**.

↓

Next, the preforms are heated in molds and blown into shape or injected into molds.

↓

The extra plastic is then trimmed off.

Glass

First a hollow is pressed or blown into the glass gob in a mold.

↓

Then air is blown into it to make the finished shape.

Caps are made separately.

Stage 3: Finishing Bottles and Jars

Plastic and glass containers may now have information printed on them.

↓

Next, the bottles and jars are cleaned, filled, and sealed.

↓

Then labels are attached, including information about the place and time of filling.

Guess What!

The first glass-making "manual" was found written on clay tablets in the library of the Assyrian king Ashurbanipal in 650 BCE.

Raw Materials for Bottles and Jars

The raw materials for glass are sand, soda ash, and limestone, which are found all around the world. Glass containers are bulky, heavy, easily broken, and expensive to transport. So most glass bottles and jars are made in many countries, close to where they will be used, largely from local materials. Some special glass bottles, however, are shipped worldwide from where they are made.

The plastics used in making bottles and jars all come from oil and gas produced by the **petrochemical industry**. Major petrochemical producers are found in the United States, western Europe, the Middle East, and Asia.

Question & Answer

What is a punt mark?

A punt mark and other markings embossed on the base of a glass bottle can show who made the bottle, which factory it came from, and information about the mold.

NORTH
AMERICA
United States
of America ◆ △ ☷

Mexico △ ☷

ATLANTIC
OCEAN

SOUTH
AMERICA

Punt marks are embossed on the bases of glass vessels.

Bottles and Jars Worldwide

Bottles and jars are made in many countries. Glass containers generally come from factories that make just glass. Plastic bottles and jars are often produced by large companies that make a range of packaging all around the world. This includes cardboard and paper cartons and boxes, and aluminum and steel cans as well.

This map shows countries that are important to the production of bottles and jars.

Key

◆ Important oil- and gas-producing countries

⍍ Important PETE-plastic-container–producing countries

⍊ Important glass-container–producing countries

Stage 1: Making Glass and Plastic

Glass and plastic are both made from raw materials mined from Earth.

Making Glass

Most container glass is made from sand, limestone, and soda ash. Sand and limestone are mined from the ground. Soda ash is mined or made in chemical factories from table salt or plants.

At the glass factory, the ingredients are weighed out into batches of about 72 percent sand, 13 percent soda ash, and 11 percent limestone, with tiny amounts of other ingredients. Large amounts of used glass, called cullet, are also added to bring down the melting temperature of the ingredients.

The batch is melted together in a furnace at more than 2732 °Fahrenheit (1500 °Celsius). The melted glass runs through channels, called forehearths, where it cools to 2012 °F (1100 °C). Then it flows into a bowl at the end of the forehearths. A plunger pushes the molten glass through an opening where it is cut into pieces called gobs.

Guess What!

Expensive crystal glass uses lead oxide instead of limestone. Glass for laboratory bottles, which must resist heat shock, has other ingredients such as boric oxide, or is made from silica (sand) alone.

When the ingredients for glass are heated, they melt together into a thick, red-hot liquid.

Nurdles are sent to factories to be made into plastic bottles and jars.

Making Plastic

To make plastic, oil and gas are first mined from underground. They are taken to a petrochemical **refinery**. There, the oil and gas **molecules** are heated in machines called reactors to break them down. These smaller molecules are then formed into long chains called polymers. Different combinations of polymers and other chemicals produce plastics with different qualities.

The raw plastic material is then made into pellets called nurdles, which are sent to plastic factories.

Question & Answer

How do ships get inside bottles?

Ships in bottles are only one form of "puzzle bottles," containing objects that look impossible to get inside bottles. The ship is carved in pieces, dropped into the bottle and put together there with special tools, glue, and a lot of patience.

17

Stage 3: Finishing Bottles and Jars

Both glass and plastic bottles and jars are checked carefully before and after labeling to make sure there are no problems. Then they may have information printed directly onto their surfaces, or labels stuck on with heat-sensitive glues. Some glass bottles have labels printed onto them with a paint that is then baked on.

Caps and other stoppers are made separately in other machines.

Question & Answer

Is glass a liquid or solid?

Somewhere in between! The structure of glass is partly like clear liquids, with molecules arranged at random. Glass molecules, however, stay still, like the molecules in solids.

Wine bottles pass through a machine that glues on the labels.

Jars are filled with cosmetic cream before being sealed.

Filling Bottles and Jars

Bottles and jars are cleaned thoroughly before they are filled. Then they are sealed before any final labels are applied. Lastly, bar codes or other information about when and where the bottles and jars were filled is printed on them. Occasionally, there are problems with spoiled or contaminated food or drink, and the place and date of filling can be traced to find out why.

Nowadays, many food and drink manufacturers have the machines to make the plastic bottles or jars they need at their factory. This saves the expense of transportation and storage.

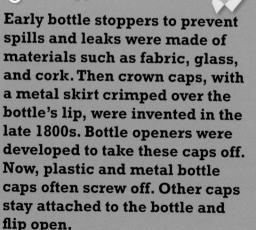

Guess What!

Early bottle stoppers to prevent spills and leaks were made of materials such as fabric, glass, and cork. Then crown caps, with a metal skirt crimped over the bottle's lip, were invented in the late 1800s. Bottle openers were developed to take these caps off. Now, plastic and metal bottle caps often screw off. Other caps stay attached to the bottle and flip open.

Packaging and Distribution

Products are packaged to protect them from shock, dust, temperature changes, and tampering during transportation. Packaging also displays the maker's brand and makes products look attractive so people will buy them.

Bottles and jars are packaging, but they also need to be packaged themselves for transporting to where they will be filled, and where they may be sold.

Most glass bottles are shipped in bulk loads. Bottles are stacked in layers separated by a sheet of plastic or heavy cardboard. Next the bulk load is strapped and stretch-wrapped, then shipped to the filling stations where the bottles are filled and put into corrugated cardboard cartons. Plastic bottles and jars are also packed in cartons. A machine then places the cartons or crates onto pallets. The pallets are all the same size so they can be stacked and stored in the least space.

Bottles are stacked up in a warehouse ready to be sent to a factory for filling.

Crates of bottled drinks are ready to be sent to shops to be sold.

Guess What!

In 1872, in Yorkshire, England, Hiram Codd designed a fizzy drink bottle that was filled upside down and sealed with a marble. Whole Codd-neck bottles are rare now, because children used to break them to get out the marble to play with.

Distribution

Most glass bottles and jars are made in special factories, and then sent by rail, road, or even sea to where they will be filled. Increasingly however, plastic bottles are made partly or completely at the factories where they will be filled.

Once the bottles and jars are filled, they are often sent to **distributors** who have the right to sell them within a certain area. Then they are taken by truck or rail to **retailers**, such as supermarkets, department stores, and gas stations, where they are sold to customers. Both glass and plastic bottles and jars are also sold over the Internet.

Marketing and Advertising

Marketing and advertising are used to promote and sell products.

Marketing

Glass and plastic containers are sold to manufacturers who need packaging for the goods that they make. The containers are sold at trade fairs where a number of manufacturers show their goods, or over the Internet.

Glass furnaces hold several tons of molten glass, so it is difficult and expensive to slow down or speed up production of glass bottles. Most glass bottles and jars are sold from stock already made, and manufacturers must plan carefully to predict how many they will need and order in advance.

Drink manufacturers need to order in advance the huge quantities of bottles they need.

Question & Answer

What is a Mason jar?

In the United States, glass Mason jars are used for preserving food. Invented by John L. Mason and sealed with flat metal lids, their size ranges from one cup to 0.3 gallons (1 litre). In Britain, preserving jars are known as Kilner jars after another inventor.

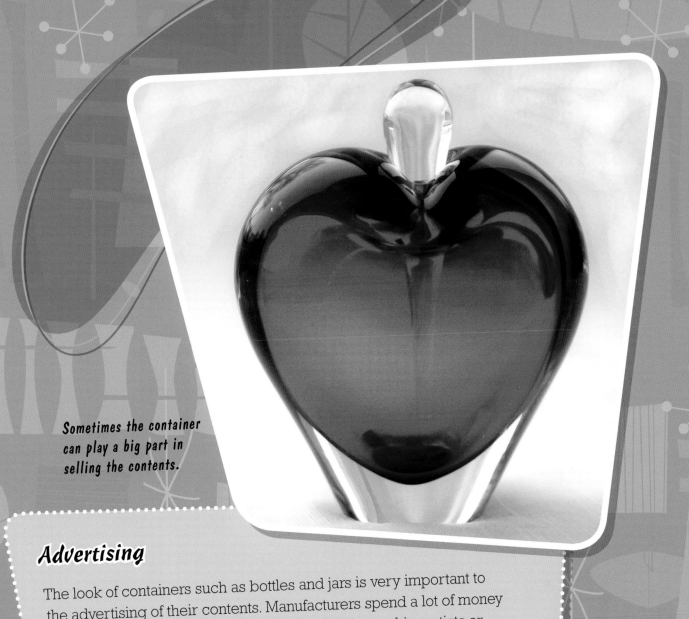

Sometimes the container can play a big part in selling the contents.

Advertising

The look of containers such as bottles and jars is very important to the advertising of their contents. Manufacturers spend a lot of money to find out what will appeal to customers. They may hire artists or designers to make their containers stand out, or even let customers help design them. The names of the products sold in bottles and jars are also very powerful, often suggesting qualities of the product. So bottles and jars are part of a whole advertising package.

Because glass containers are generally now used for luxury goods, they are often beautifully designed. People may even buy perfume as much for the elegant glass container as for the perfume itself.

Bottles and jars help advertise and sell their products. Food and drink in these containers are advertised in supermarket circulars, on television and radio, and in print ads.

Production of Bottles and Jars

Products can be made in factories in huge quantities. This is called mass production. They may also be made in small quantities by hand, by skilled craftspeople.

Mass Production

Bottles and jars are generally made in large factories that run twenty-four hours a day. In developed countries there is usually a glass factory for every one to two million people. Glass manufacturers generally make just glass.

Often plastic bottles and jars are made by packaging companies that also make cans and cardboard packaging. They make millions of the same containers at a time, and then switch to another type. Many plastic bottles and jars are made only up to a certain point at the plastic factory, as preforms. These will be expanded with heat and air to the right size and shape in small machines at the factory where they are filled.

Many large factories consist of complex machines run by very few workers.

Small-Scale Production

Almost all bottles and jars are made by machines in factories, so that they are exactly the same size and shape. There is, however, a small demand for individually made glass bottles and jars.

Older bottles and jars are treasured by collectors, who may specialize in glass bottles of a certain color, or different types such as fruit or ginger jars. They sell and swap containers at markets and meetings. Collectors also share knowledge and buy and sell on the Internet. Glass containers are more often collected, but plastic containers are also collectible, especially older or unusual ones.

Older bottles are treasured by collectors for their beauty, rarity, and history.

Question & Answer

What makes glass different colors?

Adding metals and metal oxides to glass gives different colors. Gold makes the glass a ruby red color. Copper oxide produces turquoise glass. Iron oxide and chromium create green glass. Sulfur and calcium make deep yellow, manganese produces purple, and cobalt results in deep blue glass.

Bottles and Jars and the Environment

Making any product affects the environment. It also affects the people who make the product. It is important to think about the impact of a product through its entire life cycle. This includes getting the raw materials, making the product, and disposing of it. Any problems need to be worked on so products can be made in the best ways possible.

Materials

Mining the raw materials for glass and plastic, refining the materials, and making the bottles and jars may create visual, noise, air, and water pollution. Dangers to workers include mine collapses, factory noise, and fumes. Plastic is made from **nonrenewable** oil and gas, which will eventually run out. There are also concerns that plastic food containers may leak chemicals into their contents. Companies and governments need to work together to protect workers and the environment.

Workers in plastics factories need protection against noise and fumes.

Household plastic waste is collected and compressed, ready to be recycled.

Reusing

Some glass containers are designed to be reused, often with a deposit and refund system. In countries such as Denmark and Canada, 98 percent of bottles are refillable. In developing countries such as India and Brazil, the high cost of new bottles means that manufacturers need to reuse bottles.

Recycling

Glass and plastic are both recyclable. An old glass bottle can be melted and made into a new one an unlimited number of times. Plastic containers need to be sorted into different types for recycling.

The increasing sales of bottled water have led to a waste problem with used plastic bottles. Bottling and transporting water in countries where tap water is safe is a poor use of the world's resources.

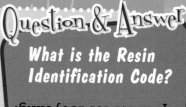

Question & Answer

What is the Resin Identification Code?

The Resin Identification Code is used all over the world to help sort different types of plastics for recycling.

Guess What!

1 PETE

Bottles and jars marked with this symbol from the Resin Identification Code are made of recyclable polyethylene terephthalate (PETE).

Questions to Think About

We need to **conserve** the raw materials used to produce even ordinary objects such as bottles and jars. Recycling materials such as glass and plastic, conserving energy, and preventing pollution as much as possible means there will be enough resources in the future and a cleaner environment.

These are some questions you might like to think about.

* What are the advantages of glass containers? What are the disadvantages?

* What are the advantages of plastic containers? What are the disadvantages?

* How can we encourage the recycling of plastic?

* How many ways of closing bottles and jars can you list? Invent a new one!

* What are some creative ways of reusing glass or plastic bottles and jars?

Do you have a favorite bottle or jar?

Glossary

conserve
To use wisely.

corked
Sealed with a plug made from cork or other materials.

cosmetics
Products for making the body seem more beautiful.

cullet
Broken or waste glass that can be melted down and recycled.

distributors
Sellers of large quantities of goods who have the right to sell a particular product in a certain area.

embossing
A raised pattern pressed into the surface as decoration.

etching
A frosted pattern made by acid eating into a surface.

flexible
Able to bend.

furnace
A very hot oven.

limestone
A common rock made mainly of calcium carbonate, formed from the skeletons of tiny sea animals.

manufacturing
Making, mainly by machine, in factories.

molds
Hollow forms in which materials can be shaped to make objects.

molecules
Groups of atoms or tiny particles that make up a substance.

molten
Heated into a liquid.

nonrenewable
Cannot easily be replaced once the supply runs out.

nurdles
Plastic pellets from which objects are made.

petrochemical industry
Manufacturers of chemical products made from petroleum oil or natural gas.

polymers
Long chains of molecules in substances such as plastic.

preforms
Partly shaped pieces of a material that will be made into objects.

preserving
Preparing something so that it lasts a long time or does not decay.

refinery
A factory where raw materials are treated to make them purer or more useful.

retailers
Stores that sell products to individual customers.

rigid
Stiff, unable to bend.

sand
Fine grains of rock and minerals, mainly silica (silicon dioxide) in the form of hard quartz.

soda ash
Sodium carbonate, a chemical produced from salt or the ash of many plants.

Index